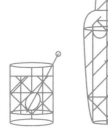

COCKTAILS

SHAKE·STIR·SIP

Publications International, Ltd.

Artwork on covers and interior and photographs on pages
13, 26, 29, 33, 35, 37, 42, 47, 49, 53, 57, 58, 77, 87,
89, 93, 111, 117, 119, 121 and 132 © Shutterstock.com.

Photographs on pages 19 and 41 © Media Bakery.

ISBN: 978-1-63938-399-3

Manufactured in China.

8 7 6 5 4 3 2 1

WARNING: Food preparation, baking and cooking involve
inherent dangers: misuse of electric products, sharp electric
tools, boiling water, hot stoves, allergic reactions, foodborne
illnesses and the like, pose numerous potential risks.
Publications International, Ltd. (PIL) assumes no responsibility
or liability for any damages you may experience as a result
of following recipes, instructions, tips or advice in this
publication.

While we hope this publication helps you find new ways
to eat delicious foods, you many not always achieve the
results desired due to variations in ingredients, cooking
temperatures, typos, errors, omissions or individual cooking
abilities.

Let's get social!

 @Publications_International

 @PublicationsInternational

www.pilbooks.com

CONTENTS

COCKTAIL
BASICS

Timeless and trendy? Yes! The wonderful world of cocktails combines the stylish classics that have been around for decades with fresh new twists that keep things exciting. You don't need to immerse yourself in cocktail culture to enjoy it, but just a little bit of basic bar knowledge will make creating great cocktails easy—and fun!

Start with the fundamentals, such as getting the right tools and stocking the bar. The following pages will show you what you'll need to prepare the recipes in this book.

STOCKING THE BAR

Buy what you like and what you'll use most. The better the ingredients, the better your drinks will be. (But do keep in mind that the most expensive ingredients aren't always the best ones.)

SPIRITS: brandy, Champagne or other sparkling wine, gin, liqueurs (almond, coffee, maraschino and orange flavors are some of the most common), rum, tequila, vodka, whiskey (bourbon, Scotch, etc.), wine (including fortified wines like port, sherry and vermouth)

MIXERS: citrus juices (fresh lemon, lime and orange), club soda, cola, ginger ale, lemon-lime soda, tomato juice (plain or spicy), tonic water, water (plain or sparkling), whipping cream

FLAVORINGS: bitters, grenadine, hot pepper sauce, salt (coarse), sugar (granulated and superfine or powdered), Worcestershire sauce

GARNISHES: lemons, limes, oranges, maraschino cherries, celery, mint sprigs, olives

BAR TOOLS

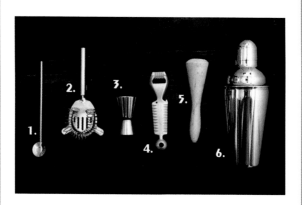

BAR SPOON: A long-handled metal spoon to stir drinks in a mixing glass or other tall glass (1).

BLENDER: A necessary tool for making ice cream drinks and slushy beverages such as frozen daiquiris, margaritas or smoothies. Also useful for crushing ice.

CHANNEL KNIFE: An inexpensive tool with a metal tooth for peeling long thin twists from citrus fruit for garnishing (4).

CITRUS JUICER: Can be anything from a simple wooden reamer or metal press to a fancy electric juicer.

COCKTAIL BASICS

CORKSCREW: A waiter's corkscrew is a popular style which includes a small blade to cut the foil from wine caps as well as a bottle opener.

JIGGER: A two-sided stainless steel measuring tool, preferably with 1- and 1½-ounce cups (3).

MIXING GLASS: A large glass (at least 16 ounces) used for shaking or stirring drinks with ice to chill them.

MUDDLER: A long, sturdy tool used to crush ingredients like herbs, fresh fruit and sugar (5).

SHAKER: A standard metal cocktail shaker is the most common style, which includes the container, a lid with a built-in strainer and a cap for the lid (6).

STRAINER: To mix drinks in a mixing glass, a Hawthorne bar strainer—flat with a spring coil around its edge—is necessary to keep the ice and muddled fruit out of your drinks (2).

OTHER KITCHEN TOOLS THAT ARE ALSO USEFUL AT THE BAR: cutting board, measuring spoons, paring knife, pitcher, tongs, vegetable peeler.

GLASSWARE

Don't worry—you don't need all of these glasses in your home bar! Think about what you like to drink and what you typically serve to guests, then purchase accordingly. (Some of them can do double duty.)

CHAMPAGNE FLUTE
4 to 10 ounces

COCKTAIL (ALSO CALLED A MARTINI GLASS)
3 to 10 ounces

COLLINS
12 to 14 ounces, taller and narrower than a highball glass, often used for drinks served over ice

COUPE
Shallow with a wide mouth

HIGHBALL
10 to 12 ounces, tall and narrow to preserve the fizz in drinks with tonic or soda water

COCKTAIL BASICS

HURRICANE
12 to 16 ounces, shaped like a hurricane lamp and used for hurricanes and other tropical drinks

MARGARITA
12 to 14 ounces, used for margaritas and daiquiris

OLD FASHIONED (ALSO CALLED A ROCKS GLASS)
4 to 8 ounces, short and wide-mouthed for spirits served neat or drinks served over ice (double old fashioned glasses hold *12 to 16 ounces*)

PILSNER GLASS
Tall, thin, flared glass used for beer or oversize drinks

SHOT GLASS
1 to 3 ounces, used for shooters and for measuring

WHITE WINE
6 to 12 ounces

RED WINE
8 to 24 ounces

GIN

GIN ST. CLEMENT'S
MAKES 1 SERVING

1½ ounces gin
1 ounce lemon juice
1 ounce orange juice
2 ounces tonic water
   Orange or lemon slice

Fill Collins or highball glass with ice; add gin, lemon juice and orange juice. Top with tonic water. Garnish with orange slice.

GIN

NEGRONI
MAKES I SERVING

1 ounce gin
1 ounce Campari
1 ounce sweet or dry vermouth
Orange slice or twist

Fill old fashioned glass half full with ice; add gin, Campari and vermouth. Stir until blended. Garnish with orange slice.

VESPER
MAKES I SERVING

3 ounces gin
1 ounce vodka
½ ounce Lillet Blanc
Lemon twist

Fill cocktail shaker with ice; add gin, vodka and Lillet Blanc. Shake until blended; strain into chilled cocktail glass. Garnish with lemon twist.

NEGRONI

FRENCH 75
MAKES 1 SERVING

- 2 ounces gin
- ½ ounce lemon juice
- 1 teaspoon superfine sugar
- 2 ounces chilled champagne or sparkling wine

Fill cocktail shaker with ice; add gin, lemon juice and sugar. Shake about 15 seconds or until cold; strain into champagne flute or coupe. Top with champagne; stir gently.

PIMM'S CUP
MAKES 1 SERVING

- 2 ounces Pimm's No. 1
  Lemon-lime soda
  Cucumber strip or spear
  Lemon twist

Fill chilled highball glass with ice; pour in Pimm's. Top with lemon-lime soda; garnish with cucumber and lemon twist.

FRENCH 75

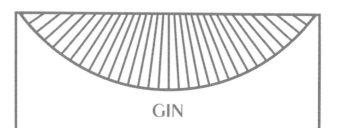

GIN

GIN SOUR
MAKES 1 SERVING

  2 ounces gin
  ¾ ounce lemon juice
  ¾ ounce simple syrup
       (recipe follows)
     Lemon twist

Fill cocktail shaker with ice; add
gin, lemon juice and simple syrup.
Shake until blended; strain into
chilled cocktail glass or coupe.
Garnish with lemon twist.

FITZGERALD: Add 2 dashes
Angostura bitters to cocktail
shaker; proceed as directed.

SIMPLE SYRUP: Combine 1 cup
water and 1 cup sugar in small
saucepan. Cook over medium heat
just until sugar is dissolved, stirring
frequently. Cool to room temperature;
store syrup in glass jar in refrigerator.

TOM COLLINS
MAKES 1 SERVING

- 2 ounces gin
- 1 ounce lemon juice
- 1 teaspoon superfine sugar
- 3 ounces chilled club soda
- Lemon slice

Fill cocktail shaker half full with ice; add gin, lemon juice and sugar. Shake until blended; strain into ice-filled Collins glass. Top with club soda. Garnish with lemon slice.

BUCK
MAKES 1 SERVING

- 1½ ounces gin
- ½ ounce lemon juice
- Ginger ale
- Lemon wedge or twist

Fill old fashioned glass with ice; add gin and lemon juice. Top with ginger ale; stir until blended. Garnish with lemon wedge.

TOM COLLINS

MARTINEZ
MAKES 1 SERVING

1½ ounces gin
¾ ounce sweet vermouth
½ ounce maraschino liqueur
2 dashes orange bitters
   Lemon or orange twist

Fill mixing glass or cocktail shaker with ice; add gin, vermouth, liqueur and bitters. Stir about 20 seconds or until very cold; strain into chilled coupe or cocktail glass. Garnish with lemon twist.

RAMOS GIN FIZZ
MAKES 1 SERVING

2	ounces gin
1	ounce whipping cream
½	ounce lemon juice
½	ounce lime juice
1	teaspoon superfine sugar
2	dashes orange flower water
1	egg white
	Chilled club soda

Combine gin, cream, lemon juice, lime juice, sugar, orange flower water and egg white in cocktail shaker; shake without ice 30 seconds. Add 1 cup ice cubes to shaker; shake about 20 seconds or until cold. Strain into chilled highball or Collins glass; top with club soda.

NOTE: A Ramos Gin Fizz is typically not served over ice, but if you don't have a chilled glass, adding a few ice cubes will help keep the drink cold longer (although it will also dilute the drink).

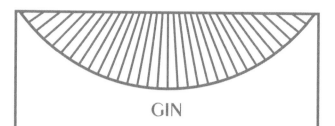

TUXEDO COCKTAIL
MAKES 1 SERVING

1½ ounces gin
1 ounce dry vermouth
½ teaspoon maraschino liqueur
¼ teaspoon absinthe or Pernod
2 dashes orange bitters
Maraschino cherry

Fill mixing glass or cocktail shaker with ice; add gin, vermouth, liqueur, absinthe and bitters. Stir until very cold; strain into chilled cocktail glass. Garnish with maraschino cherry.

VODKA

COSMOPOLITAN
MAKES 1 SERVING

- 2 ounces vodka or lemon vodka
- 1 ounce triple sec
- 1 ounce cranberry juice
- ½ ounce lime juice
- Lemon twist

Fill cocktail shaker half full with ice; add vodka, triple sec and juices. Shake until blended; strain into chilled cocktail glass. Garnish with lemon twist.

BLOODY MARY

MAKES 1 SERVING

1 dash *each* Worcestershire sauce, hot pepper sauce, celery salt, black pepper and salt

3 ounces tomato juice

1½ ounces vodka

½ ounce lemon juice

Celery stalk with leaves, pickle spear, lemon slice and/or green olives

Fill highball glass with ice; add dashes of Worcestershire sauce, hot pepper sauce, celery salt, black pepper and salt. Add tomato juice, vodka and lemon juice; stir until blended. Serve with desired garnishes.

CHERRY COLLINS

MAKES 1 SERVING

2 ounces cherry-flavored vodka

¾ ounce lemon juice

¾ ounce simple syrup
(recipe follows)

Club soda

Fresh cherries

Fill highball glass with ice; add vodka, lemon juice and simple syrup. Stir until blended; top with club soda. Garnish with cherries.

SIMPLE SYRUP: Combine 1 cup water and 1 cup sugar in small saucepan. Cook over medium heat just until sugar is dissolved, stirring frequently. Cool to room temperature; store syrup in glass jar in refrigerator.

MOSCOW MULE

MAKES 1 SERVING

½ lime, cut into 2 wedges
1½ ounces vodka
4 to 6 ounces chilled ginger beer
Lime slice and fresh mint sprig

Fill copper mug or Collins glass half full with ice. Squeeze lime juice over ice; drop lime wedges into mug. Pour vodka over ice; top with beer. Garnish with lime slice and mint sprig.

HARVEY WALLBANGER

MAKES 1 SERVING

3 ounces vodka
6 ounces orange juice
1 ounce Galliano
Orange slice

Fill highball glass half full with ice; pour vodka over ice. Stir in orange juice. Pour Galliano over top (do not stir). Garnish with orange slice.

MOSCOW MULE

LEMON DROP
MAKES I SERVING

- 1 teaspoon sugar (optional)
- 2 ounces vodka
- ¾ ounce lemon juice
- ½ ounce simple syrup (recipe follows)
- Lemon twist

Moisten rim of chilled cocktail or shot glass; dip in sugar, if desired. Fill cocktail shaker half full with ice; add vodka, lemon juice and simple syrup. Shake until blended; strain into glass. Garnish with lemon twist.

SIMPLE SYRUP: Combine 1 cup water and 1 cup sugar in small saucepan. Cook over medium heat just until sugar is dissolved, stirring frequently. Cool to room temperature; store syrup in glass jar in refrigerator.

VODKA

BLACK RUSSIAN
MAKES 1 SERVING

2 ounces vodka
1 ounce coffee liqueur

Fill old fashioned or cocktail glass with ice; add vodka and liqueur. Stir until blended.

WHITE RUSSIAN: Float 1 tablespoon whipping cream over top of Black Russian.

SEA BREEZE
MAKES 1 SERVING

3 ounces cranberry juice
2 ounces grapefruit juice
1½ ounces vodka
   Lemon slice

Fill cocktail shaker half full with ice; add cranberry juice, grapefruit juice and vodka. Shake until blended; strain into ice-filled Collins or highball glass. Garnish with lemon slice.

BLACK RUSSIAN

WEST SIDE
MAKES 1 SERVING

- 2 ounces lemon vodka
- 1 ounce lemon juice
- ½ ounce simple syrup (recipe follows)
- 1 sprig fresh mint
  Chilled club soda

Fill cocktail shaker with ice; add vodka, lemon juice, simple syrup and mint. Shake until blended. Top with splash of club soda; strain into chilled coupe or cocktail glass.

SIMPLE SYRUP: Combine 1 cup water and 1 cup sugar in small saucepan. Cook over medium heat just until sugar is dissolved, stirring frequently. Cool to room temperature; store syrup in glass jar in refrigerator.

ELECTRIC LEMONADE
MAKES 1 SERVING

2 ounces sweet and sour mix
1½ ounces vodka
½ ounce blue curaçao
　Lemon-lime soda
　Lime wedges

Fill Collins glass half full with ice; add sweet and sour mix, vodka and curaçao. Top with soda. Garnish with lime wedges.

SALTY DOG
MAKES 1 SERVING

6 ounces grapefruit juice
　Salt
1½ ounces vodka

Moisten rim of highball glass with grapefruit juice; dip in salt. Fill glass with ice; pour vodka over ice. Stir in grapefruit juice.

GREYHOUND: Omit salt.

ELECTRIC LEMONADE

WHISKEY

SAZERAC

- 2 ounces whiskey
- ¼ ounce anise-flavored liqueur
- ½ ounce simple syrup (page 50)
- Dash of bitters
- Lemon twist

Fill cocktail shaker half full with ice; add whiskey, liqueur, syrup and bitters. Stir until blended; strain into old fashioned glass. Garnish with lemon twist.

RATTLESNAKE
MAKES I SERVING

2 ounces whiskey
½ ounce lemon juice
¾ teaspoon powdered sugar
1 dash absinthe or Pernod
1 egg white

Fill cocktail shaker with ice; add whiskey, lemon juice, powdered sugar, absinthe and egg white. Shake until frothy; strain into chilled coupe or cocktail glass.

AMBER JACK
MAKES I SERVING

2 ounces sweet and sour mix
1 ounce Tennessee whiskey
½ ounce amaretto
Maraschino cherry

Fill cocktail shaker with ice; add sweet and sour mix, whiskey and amaretto. Shake until blended; strain into chilled cocktail glass. Garnish with maraschino cherry.

RATTLESNAKE

GODFATHER
MAKES 1 SERVING

1½ ounces Scotch
½ ounce amaretto
   Orange slice or twist

Fill mixing glass or cocktail shaker half full with ice; add Scotch and amaretto. Stir about 20 seconds or until cold; strain into ice-filled old fashioned glass. Garnish with orange slice.

MANHATTAN
MAKES 1 SERVING

2 ounces whiskey
1 ounce sweet vermouth
1 dash Angostura bitters
   Maraschino cherry

Fill mixing glass or cocktail shaker half full with ice; add whiskey, vermouth and bitters. Stir until blended; strain into chilled cocktail glass or ice-filled old fashioned glass. Garnish with maraschino cherry.

GODFATHER

SCOFFLAW

MAKES I SERVING

1½ ounces rye whiskey
1 ounce dry vermouth
¾ ounce lemon juice
¾ ounce grenadine
2 dashes orange bitters

Fill cocktail shaker with ice; add whiskey, vermouth, lemon juice, grenadine and bitters. Shake until blended; strain into chilled coupe or cocktail glass.

RUSTY NAIL

MAKES I SERVING

1½ ounces Scotch
1 ounce Drambuie

Fill old fashioned glass with ice; add Scotch and Drambuie. Stir until blended.

SCOFFLAW

WHISKEY SMASH
MAKES 1 SERVING

2 lemon quarters

8 fresh mint leaves,
plus additional for garnish

½ ounce simple syrup
(recipe follows)

2 ounces bourbon

Muddle lemon quarters, 8 mint leaves and simple syrup in cocktail shaker. Add bourbon; shake until blended. Strain into old fashioned glass filled with crushed ice. Garnish with additional mint.

SIMPLE SYRUP: Combine 1 cup water and 1 cup sugar in small saucepan. Cook over medium heat just until sugar is dissolved, stirring frequently. Cool to room temperature; store syrup in glass jar in refrigerator.

BOULEVARDIER
MAKES 1 SERVING

1½ ounces bourbon
1 ounce sweet vermouth
1 ounce Campari
   Orange slice or twist

Fill mixing glass or cocktail shaker half full with ice; add bourbon, vermouth and Campari. Stir 30 seconds or until cold; strain into chilled old fashioned or cocktail glass. Garnish with orange slice.

ROB ROY
MAKES 1 SERVING

1½ ounces Scotch or other whiskey
¼ ounce sweet vermouth
   Dash of bitters
   Maraschino cherry

Fill mixing glass or cocktail shaker half full with ice; add Scotch, vermouth and bitters. Stir until blended; strain into chilled cocktail glass. Garnish with maraschino cherry.

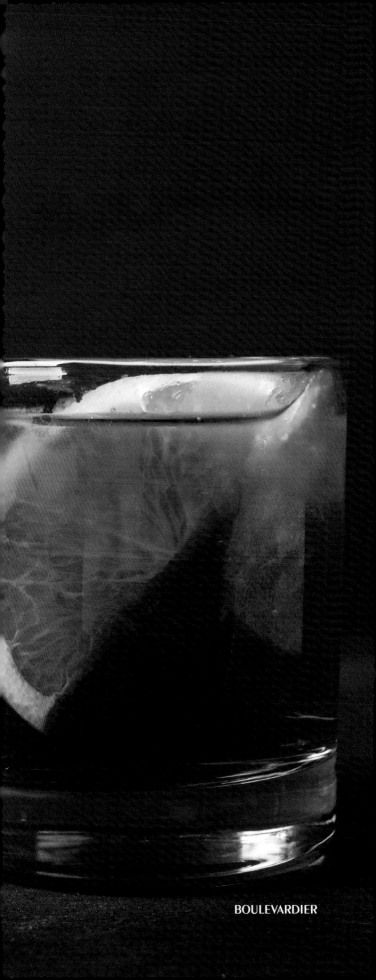

BOULEVARDIER

HOT TODDY
MAKES 2 SERVINGS

- 2 lemon wedges
- 2 teaspoons honey or sugar
- 1½ cups hot brewed tea or hot water
- 3 ounces whiskey or brandy
- 2 cinnamon sticks
- Lemon slices

Squeeze lemon wedges into two warmed Irish coffee glasses or mugs; stir in honey. Stir in hot tea and whiskey with cinnamon sticks. Garnish with lemon slices.

HUNTER'S COCKTAIL
MAKES 1 SERVING

- 1½ ounces rye whiskey
- ½ ounce cherry brandy
- Maraschino cherry

Fill old fashioned glass half full with ice; add whiskey and brandy. Stir until blended. Garnish with maraschino cherry.

HOT TODDY

WHISKEY SOUR
MAKES 1 SERVING

2 ounces whiskey

Juice of ½ lemon

1 teaspoon powdered sugar *or* 1 tablespoon simple syrup (page 50)

Lemon slice and maraschino cherry

Fill cocktail shaker half full with ice; add whiskey, lemon juice and powdered sugar. Shake until blended; strain into ice-filled old fashioned glass. Garnish with lemon slice and maraschino cherry.

VARIATION: Fill cocktail shaker half full with ice; add 4 ounces sweet and sour mix and 1½ ounces whiskey. Shake until blended; strain into ice-filled old fashioned glass. Garnish with lemon slice and maraschino cherry.

TEQUILA

TEQUILA SUNRISE
MAKES I SERVING

- 2 ounces tequila
- 6 ounces orange juice
- 1 tablespoon grenadine
  Orange slice and maraschino cherry

Place 4 ice cubes in hurricane or highball glass. Pour tequila and orange juice over ice (do not stir). Pour in grenadine; let sink to bottom of glass (do not stir). Garnish with orange slice and maraschino cherry.

CLASSIC MARGARITA
MAKES 2 SERVINGS

Lime wedges
Coarse salt
4 ounces tequila
2 ounces triple sec
2 ounces lime juice

1. Rub rim of two margarita glasses with lime wedges; dip in salt.

2. Fill cocktail shaker with ice; add tequila, triple sec and lime juice. Shake until blended; strain into glasses. Garnish with lime wedges.

FROZEN MARGARITA: Rub rim of margarita glasses with lime wedges; dip in salt. Combine tequila, triple sec, lime juice and 2 cups ice in blender; blend until smooth. Pour into glasses; garnish with lime wedges.

EL DORADO
MAKES 1 SERVING

- 2 ounces tequila
- 1 tablespoon honey
- 1½ ounces lemon juice
- Lemon or orange slice

Fill cocktail shaker half full with ice; add tequila, honey and lemon juice. Shake until blended; strain into ice-filled old fashioned or Collins glass. Garnish with lemon slice.

TEQUILA MATADOR
MAKES 1 SERVING

- 1½ ounces tequila blanco (silver)
- 1 ounce pineapple juice
- ½ ounce lime juice
- Lime or pineapple wedge

Fill cocktail shaker with ice; add tequila, pineapple juice and lime juice. Shake until blended; strain into champagne flute or ice-filled old fashioned glass. Garnish with lime wedge.

EL DORADO

CANTARITO
MAKES 1 SERVING

Lime wedge
Coarse salt
1½ ounces tequila
½ ounce lime juice
½ ounce lemon juice
½ ounce orange juice
Grapefruit soda
Lime, lemon and/or orange
  wedges

Rub rim of Collins glass with lime wedge; dip in salt. Fill glass with ice; add tequila, lime juice, lemon juice and orange juice. Top with grapefruit soda; stir until blended. Garnish with citrus wedges.

NOTE: In Mexico, Cantaritos are typically served in salt-rimmed clay pots.

ECLIPSE

MAKES 1 SERVING

- 2 ounces tequila añejo
- ¾ ounce Aperol
- ¾ ounce cherry liqueur
- ¾ ounce lemon juice
- ¼ ounce mezcal
- Lemon twist

Fill cocktail shaker with ice; add tequila, Aperol, liqueur, lemon juice and mezcal. Shake until blended; strain into coupe or old fashioned glass. Garnish with lemon twist.

BRAVE BULL

MAKES 1 SERVING

- 1½ ounces tequila
- 1 ounce coffee liqueur
- Lemon twist

Fill chilled old fashioned glass with ice; add tequila and liqueur. Stir until blended. Garnish with lemon twist.

ECLIPSE

MANZARITA
MAKES 1 SERVING

2 lemon quarters

⅛ teaspoon ground cinnamon

2 ounces tequila blanco
(white or silver)

1½ ounces apple cider (nonalcoholic)

¾ ounce elderflower liqueur

Cinnamon stick

Muddle lemon quarters and
cinnamon in cocktail shaker.
Fill shaker half full with ice; add
tequila, cider and liqueur. Shake
until blended; strain into ice-filled
old fashioned glass. Garnish with
cinnamon stick.

BRANDY

BRANDY COLLINS
MAKES I SERVING

- 2 ounces brandy
- 1 ounce lemon juice
- 1 teaspoon powdered sugar
- 3 ounces chilled club soda
  Orange slice and maraschino
  cherry

Fill cocktail shaker half full with
ice; add brandy, lemon juice
and powdered sugar. Shake until
blended; strain into ice-filled Collins
glass. Add club soda; stir until
blended. Garnish with orange
slice and maraschino cherry.

CRANBERRY CAIPIRINHA
MAKES I SERVING

2 lime wedges
1 orange wedge
12 fresh cranberries
2 tablespoons packed brown sugar
2 ounces cachaça
1 ounce cranberry juice
   Lime twist or slice

Muddle lime wedges, orange wedge, cranberries and brown sugar in cocktail shaker. Add cachaça and cranberry juice; shake until blended. Strain into ice-filled old fashioned glass; garnish with lime twist.

FRENCH CONNECTION
MAKES I SERVING

1 ½ ounces cognac

¾ ounce amaretto

Fill old fashioned glass with ice; add cognac and amaretto. Stir until blended.

FRENCH CONNECTION NO. 2: Substitute orange liqueur for the amaretto.

SIDECAR
MAKES I SERVING

2 ounces brandy or cognac

2 ounces orange-flavored liqueur

½ ounce lemon juice

Fill cocktail shaker half full with ice; add brandy, liqueur and lemon juice. Shake until blended; strain into chilled cocktail glass.

FRENCH CONNECTION

PISCO SOUR
MAKES 1 SERVING

2   ounces pisco
1   ounce lime juice
¼   ounce simple syrup
     (recipe follows)
½   egg white
1   dash Angostura bitters

Fill cocktail shaker half full with ice; add pisco, lime juice, simple syrup and egg white. Shake until blended; strain into chilled cocktail glass. Sprinkle foam with bitters.

SIMPLE SYRUP: Combine 1 cup water and 1 cup sugar in small saucepan. Cook over medium heat just until sugar is dissolved, stirring frequently. Cool to room temperature; store syrup in glass jar in refrigerator.

JACK ROSE
MAKES I SERVING

2 ounces applejack
¾ ounce lime juice
¾ ounce grenadine
  Lime slice or wedge

Fill cocktail shaker with ice; add applejack, lime juice and grenadine. Shake about 15 seconds or until cold; strain into chilled cocktail glass or coupe. Garnish with lime slice.

STINGER
MAKES I SERVING

2 ounces brandy
¾ ounce white crème de menthe

Fill cocktail shaker half full with ice; add brandy and crème de menthe. Shake until blended; strain into chilled cocktail glass.

JACK ROSE

HOT MULLED CIDER

MAKES 8 SERVINGS

4 cups (1 quart) apple cider

¼ cup packed brown sugar

1 teaspoon balsamic or
    cider vinegar

½ teaspoon vanilla

1 cinnamon stick

3 whole cloves

¼ cup applejack or bourbon

Combine apple cider, brown sugar, vinegar, vanilla, cinnamon stick and cloves in large saucepan; bring to a boil over medium-high heat. Reduce heat to low; simmer 30 minutes. Remove and discard cinnamon stick and cloves. Stir in applejack. Serve warm.

VICEROY
MAKES 1 SERVING

1½ ounces pisco

1 ounce Lillet Blanc

½ ounce lime juice

½ ounce simple syrup
(recipe follows)

1½ ounces tonic water

Fresh mint sprig

Combine pisco, Lillet Blanc, lime juice and simple syrup in ice-filled highball glass. Top with tonic water; stir until blended. Garnish with mint sprig.

SIMPLE SYRUP: Combine 1 cup water and 1 cup sugar in small saucepan. Cook over medium heat just until sugar is dissolved, stirring frequently. Cool to room temperature; store syrup in glass jar in refrigerator.

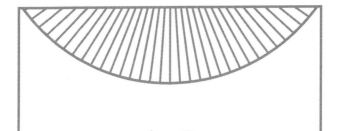

RUM

MOJITO
MAKES 2 SERVINGS

- 8 fresh mint leaves, plus additional for garnish
- 2 ounces lime juice
- 2 teaspoons superfine sugar or powdered sugar
- 3 ounces light rum
  Chilled club soda or seltzer
- 2 lime slices

Combine half of mint leaves, lime juice and sugar in each of two highball glasses; mash with wooden spoon or muddler. Fill glasses with ice. Pour rum over ice; top with club soda. Garnish with lime slices and additional mint leaves.

HAVANA SPECIAL
MAKES 1 SERVING

2 ounces pineapple juice
1½ ounces light rum
¼ ounce maraschino liqueur
Pineapple slice

Fill cocktail shaker half full with ice; add pineapple juice, rum and liqueur. Shake until blended; strain into ice-filled snifter or highball glass. Garnish with pineapple slice.

CASABLANCA
MAKES 1 SERVING

1½ ounces white rum
½ ounce orange liqueur
¼ ounce maraschino liqueur
½ ounce lime juice

Fill cocktail shaker with ice; add rum, liqueurs and lime juice. Shake until blended; strain into chilled cocktail glass.

HAVANA SPECIAL

DAIQUIRI
MAKES 1 SERVING

1½ ounces light rum

¾ ounce lime juice

¼ ounce simple syrup
(recipe follows) *or*
1 teaspoon powdered sugar

Lime wedge

Fill cocktail shaker half full with ice; add rum, lime juice and simple syrup. Shake until blended; strain into chilled cocktail glass or margarita glass. Garnish with lime wedge.

SIMPLE SYRUP: Combine 1 cup water and 1 cup sugar in small saucepan. Cook over medium heat just until sugar is dissolved, stirring frequently. Cool to room temperature; store syrup in glass jar in refrigerator.

RUM SWIZZLE
MAKES 1 SERVING

- 2 ounces rum
- 1 ounce lime juice
- 1 teaspoon superfine sugar
- 2 dashes Angostura bitters
  Lime slice

Combine rum, lime juice, sugar and bitters in chilled Collins or highball glass filled with crushed ice; stir vigorously with long spoon until blended. Garnish with lime slice.

NOTE: Swizzles originated in the Caribbean in the early 1800's. These tall rum drinks were served over crushed ice and mixed with long twigs; the twigs were rubbed rapidly between one's hands, which was called "swizzling." Most swizzle drinks today are mixed with long bar spoons and they can contain spirits other than rum.

COCO LOCO
MAKES 1 SERVING

4 ounces pineapple juice
2 ounces light rum
1 ounce cream of coconut
1 ounce milk
½ ounce amaretto
1 teaspoon grenadine
½ cup ice cubes
   Pineapple slice and/or
      maraschino cherry

Combine pineapple juice, rum, cream of coconut, milk, amaretto, grenadine and ice in blender; blend until smooth. Serve in wine glass or hollowed-out coconut. Garnish with pineapple slice.

JUNGLE BIRD
MAKES 1 SERVING

- 1½ ounces Jamaican or dark aged rum
- 1½ ounces pineapple juice
- ¾ ounce Campari
- ½ ounce lime juice
- ½ ounce simple syrup (recipe follows)
- Pineapple wedge

Fill cocktail shaker with ice; add rum, pineapple juice, Campari, lime juice and simple syrup. Shake 30 seconds or until cold; strain into ice-filled old fashioned glass, copper mug or tiki mug. Garnish with pineapple wedge.

SIMPLE SYRUP: Combine 1 cup water and 1 cup sugar in small saucepan. Cook over medium heat just until sugar is dissolved, stirring frequently. Cool to room temperature; store syrup in glass jar in refrigerator.

BEACHCOMBER
MAKES 1 SERVING

2 ounces light rum
1 ounce orange liqueur
1 ounce lime juice
¼ ounce maraschino liqueur
  Maraschino cherry

Fill cocktail shaker with ice; add rum, orange liqueur, lime juice and maraschino liqueur. Shake until blended; strain into chilled cocktail glass. Garnish with maraschino cherry.

DARK AND STORMY
MAKES 1 SERVING

4 ounces ginger beer
2 ounces dark rum
½ ounce lime juice

Fill old fashioned or Collins glass with ice; add ginger beer, rum and lime juice. Stir until blended.

BEACHCOMBER

LIQUEURS

DON PEDRO
MAKES 1 SERVING

1 cup vanilla ice cream
2 ounces whipping cream
1 ounce whiskey
1 ounce coffee liqueur

Combine ice cream, cream, whiskey and liqueur in blender; blend until smooth. Serve in hurricane glass.

GOLDEN DREAM
MAKES 1 SERVING

- 2 ounces orange liqueur
- 2 ounces Galliano
- 2 ounces orange juice
- 1 ounce whipping cream

Fill cocktail shaker half full with ice; add liqueur, Galliano, orange juice and cream. Shake 30 seconds or until well blended; strain into chilled cocktail glass.

GRASSHOPPER
MAKES 1 SERVING

- 2 ounces crème de menthe
- 2 ounces crème de cacao
- 2 ounces half-and-half or whipping cream

Fill cocktail shaker half full with ice; add crème de menthe, crème de cacao and half-and-half. Shake until blended; strain into chilled cocktail glass.

GOLDEN DREAM

SWEET RUBY
MAKES I SERVING

- 1 ounce ruby port
- ¾ ounce amaretto
- 2 dashes Angostura bitters

Fill mixing glass or cocktail shaker with ice; add port, amaretto and bitters. Stir 10 seconds; strain into chilled old fashioned glass half full with ice.

AMARETTO STONE SOUR
MAKES I SERVING

- 2 ounces amaretto
- 2 ounces sweet and sour mix
- 2 ounces orange juice
  Maraschino cherry

Fill highball glass with ice; add amaretto, sweet and sour mix and orange juice. Stir until blended. Garnish with maraschino cherry.

SWEET RUBY

LAST WORD

MAKES 1 SERVING

- ¾ ounce gin
- ¾ ounce green Chartreuse
- ¾ ounce maraschino liqueur
- ¾ ounce lime juice
- Lime twist

Fill cocktail shaker with ice; add gin, Chartreuse, liqueur and lime juice. Shake until blended; strain into chilled coupe or cocktail glass. Garnish with lime twist.

B-52

MAKES 1 SERVING

- ½ ounce coffee liqueur
- ½ ounce Irish cream liqueur
- ½ ounce orange liqueur

Pour coffee liqueur into shot glass; top with Irish cream liqueur, then orange liqueur (do not stir).

LAST WORD

WHITE LINEN
MAKES 1 SERVING

1½ ounces gin

1 ounce lemon juice

½ ounce elderflower liqueur

½ ounce simple syrup
(recipe follows)

Chilled club soda

Lemon slice

Fill cocktail shaker with ice; add gin, lemon juice, liqueur and simple syrup. Shake until blended; strain into ice-filled Collins or highball glass. Top with club soda. Garnish with lemon slice.

SIMPLE SYRUP: Combine 1 cup water and 1 cup sugar in small saucepan. Cook over medium heat just until sugar is dissolved, stirring frequently. Cool to room temperature; store syrup in glass jar in refrigerator.

BLOOD AND SAND
MAKES 1 SERVING

1 ounce Scotch
¾ ounce cherry liqueur
¾ ounce sweet vermouth
¾ ounce orange juice
   Maraschino cherry

Fill cocktail shaker with ice; add Scotch, liqueur, vermouth and orange juice. Shake 15 seconds or until cold; strain into chilled coupe or cocktail glass. Garnish with maraschino cherry.

MUDSLIDE
MAKES 1 SERVING

1 ounce vodka
1 ounce coffee liqueur
1 ounce Irish cream liqueur

Fill cocktail shaker half full with ice; add vodka, coffee liqueur and Irish cream liqueur. Shake until blended; strain into chilled cocktail glass.

BLOOD AND SAND

FUZZY NAVEL
MAKES 1 SERVING

4 ounces orange juice
1½ ounces peach schnapps
1 ounce vodka (optional)
   Peach or orange slice

Fill cocktail shaker half full with ice; add orange juice, schnapps and vodka, if desired. Shake until blended; strain into ice-filled glass. Garnish with peach slice.

KAMIKAZE
MAKES 1 SERVING

1 ounce vodka
1 ounce triple sec
1 ounce lime juice

Fill cocktail shaker half full with ice; add vodka, triple sec and lime juice. Shake until blended; strain into chilled cocktail glass, large shot glass or ice-filled old fashioned glass.

FUZZY NAVEL

BEER & CIDER

MICHELADA CUBANA
MAKES 1 SERVING

- 1 lime wedge
- Coarse salt
- 2 tablespoons lime juice
- 1 teaspoon Worcestershire sauce
- 1 teaspoon hot pepper sauce
- ½ teaspoon Maggi seasoning or soy sauce
- 6 ounces chilled Mexican pale lager

Rub rim of beer glass with lime wedge; dip in salt. Fill glass with ice; add lime juice, Worcestershire sauce, hot pepper sauce and Maggi seasoning. Top with beer. Garnish with lime wedge.

BLACK VELVET
MAKES 1 SERVING

3 ounces chilled champagne

3 ounces chilled stout

Pour champagne into champagne flute; slowly top with stout.

TIP: For tall glasses, use 4 ounces of each beverage. For pint glasses, use 6 ounces of each.

STONE FENCE
MAKES 1 SERVING

2 ounces dark rum, rye whiskey or applejack

6 ounces hard cider

Lemon twist

Pour rum into pint glass or old fashioned glass; add 2 to 4 ice cubes. Top with cider; stir until blended. Garnish with lemon twist.

BLACK VELVET

SNAKE BITE
MAKES 1 SERVING

8 ounces ale
8 ounces hard cider

Pour ale into chilled pint glass;
top with cider (do not stir).

CIDER SANGRIA
MAKES 4 SERVINGS

1 cup apple cider (nonalcoholic)
⅓ cup apple brandy
2 tablespoons lemon juice
1 apple, thinly sliced
1 pear, thinly sliced
1 orange, quartered and
  thinly sliced
1 bottle (22 ounces) chilled
  hard cider

Combine apple cider, apple brandy,
lemon juice, apple, pear and orange
slices in large pitcher; stir until
blended. Just before serving, stir
in hard cider. Serve over ice.

SNAKE BITE

SHANDY
MAKES I SERVING

6 ounces chilled beer

6 ounces chilled carbonated lemonade, lemon-lime soda, ginger beer or ginger ale

Lemon slice

Pour beer into chilled large wine glass or pint glass; top with lemonade. Garnish with lemon slice.

BLOODY BEER
MAKES I SERVING

Lime wedge (optional)

Coarse salt or celery salt (optional)

3 ounces Bloody Mary mix, tomato juice or tomato-clam juice

1 can or bottle (12 ounces) chilled lager beer

Rub rim of pint glass with lime wedge; dip in salt, if desired. Pour Bloody Mary mix into glass; top with lager.

SHANDY

THE CURE
MAKES 1 SERVING

5 ounces light-colored lager
1 ounce ginger liqueur
½ ounce lemon juice
  Lemon slices and fresh mint sprig

Fill highball or Collins glass with ice. Add lager, liqueur and lemon juice; stir until blended. Garnish with lemon slices and mint sprig.

HALF-AND-HALF
MAKES 1 SERVING

8 ounces ale
8 ounces porter

Pour ale into chilled pint glass. Pour porter over back of spoon on top of ale (do not stir).

THE CURE

WINE & CHAMPAGNE

POMEGRANATE MIMOSA
MAKES 8 SERVINGS

- 2 cups chilled pomegranate juice
- 1 bottle (750 ml) chilled champagne
- Pomegranate seeds

Pour pomegranate juice into eight champagne flutes; top with champagne. Garnish with pomegranate seeds.

SHERRY COBBLER
MAKES 1 SERVING

- ½ teaspoon orange liqueur
- ½ teaspoon simple syrup (recipe follows)
- 4 ounces dry sherry (amontillado or oloroso)

  Orange slice

Fill large wine glass or old fashioned glass three-fourths full with crushed ice. Add liqueur and simple syrup; stir until blended. Stir in sherry. Garnish with orange slice.

SIMPLE SYRUP: Combine 1 cup water and 1 cup sugar in small saucepan. Cook over medium heat just until sugar is dissolved, stirring frequently. Cool to room temperature; store syrup in glass jar in refrigerator.

APPLE CIDER MIMOSA
MAKES I SERVING

3 ounces chilled apple cider (nonalcoholic)

3 ounces chilled champagne

Apple slice

Pour cider into champagne flute; top with champagne. Garnish with apple slice.

APEROL SPRITZ
MAKES I SERVING

3 ounces Prosecco or sparkling wine

1½ ounces Aperol

Chilled club soda or sparkling water

Orange slice

Fill wine glass or highball glass half full with ice. Add Prosecco, Aperol and splash of club soda; stir gently. Garnish with orange slice.

APPLE CIDER MIMOSA

MOONWALK
MAKES I SERVING

1 ounce grapefruit juice

1 ounce orange liqueur

3 drops rosewater*

Chilled champagne or
sparkling wine

*Rosewater can be found at many liquor
stores and supermarkets as well as Middle
Eastern grocery stores.

Fill cocktail shaker half full with ice;
add grapefruit juice, liqueur and
rosewater. Shake until blended;
strain into champagne flute. Top
with champagne.

BLUSHING BRIDE
MAKES I SERVING

1 ounce peach schnapps

1 ounce grenadine

4 ounces chilled champagne

Combine schnapps and grenadine
in champagne flute; top with
champagne. Stir until blended.

MOONWALK

MIMOSA
MAKES 4 SERVINGS

2 cups chilled orange juice
1 cup chilled champagne
Orange wedges

Pour orange juice into four champagne flutes; top with champagne. Garnish with orange wedges.

MULLED WINE
MAKES 6 TO 8 SERVINGS

½ gallon (8 cups) wine
6 cardamom pods
3 cinnamon sticks
3 whole star anise
3 whole cloves

Combine wine, cardamom pods, cinnamon sticks, star anise and cloves in large saucepan; heat until warm (do not boil). Remove or strain out spices before serving.

MIMOSA

MOCKTAILS

CRANBERRY LIME RICKY
MAKES 1 SERVING

- 4 ounces cranberry juice
- 2 tablespoons grenadine
- 2 tablespoons lime juice
- 4 ounces chilled seltzer
     Lime wedge and fresh cranberries

Pour cranberry juice, grenadine and lime juice into ice-filled Collins or highball glass; stir until blended. Stir in seltzer. Garnish with lime wedge and cranberries.

CARDAMOM-SPIKED LEMONADE SPRITZER

MAKES 6 SERVINGS

3	cups water
1¼	cups sugar
40	whole white cardamom pods, cracked
2	cups lemon juice
1	bottle (750 ml) Asti Spumante or club soda
	Fresh mint sprig

1. Combine water, sugar and cardamom pods in medium saucepan; bring to a simmer over high heat. Cook and stir until sugar dissolves. Reduce heat to low; cover and simmer 30 minutes. Remove from heat; cool completely. Refrigerate 2 hours or up to 3 days.

2. Pour mixture through strainer into 3-quart pitcher; discard cardamom pods. Stir in lemon juice and Asti Spumante. Serve over ice. Garnish with mint sprig.

CUCUMBER PUNCH
MAKES 10 SERVINGS

1 English cucumber, thinly sliced
1 cup water
½ (12-ounce) can thawed frozen
   limeade concentrate
1 bottle (1 liter) chilled club soda
   Lime wedges

1. Combine cucumber slices, water and limeade concentrate in punch bowl or pitcher. Refrigerate 1 hour.

2. Just before serving, stir in club soda and ice. Pour into ice-filled old fashioned or highball glasses. Garnish with lime wedges.

PINEAPPLE AGUA FRESCA
MAKES 6 SERVINGS

⅓ plus ¼ cup sugar, divided

3 cups fresh pineapple chunks (about half of 1 large pineapple)

¼ cup lime juice

2 tablespoons chopped fresh mint

2 cups chilled club soda

Fresh mint sprig

1. Place ¼ cup sugar in shallow dish. Wet rims of six glasses with damp paper towel; dip in sugar.

2. Combine pineapple, remaining ⅓ cup sugar, lime juice and chopped mint in blender; blend 30 seconds to 1 minute or until frothy.

3. Pour into pitcher; stir in club soda. Serve immediately over ice. Garnish with mint.

INDEX

INDEX

INDEX

INDEX

CONVERSION CHARTS

¼ ounce = ½ tablespoon

½ ounce = 1 tablespoon

¾ ounce = 1½ tablespoons

1 ounce = 2 tablespoons

2 ounces = ¼ cup

4 ounces = ½ cup

6 ounces = ¾ cup

8 ounces = 1 cup

16 ounces = 2 cups

24 ounces = 3 cups

32 ounces = 1 quart

VOLUME EQUIVALENTS (LIQUID)

US STANDARD	US STANDARD (OUNCES)	METRIC (APPROXIMATE)
2 tablespoons	1 fluid ounce	30 mL
½ cup	4 fluid ounces	125 mL
1 cup	8 fluid ounces	250 mL
1½ cups	12 fluid ounces	375 mL
2 cups	16 fluid ounces	500 mL